A Pocket Guide to Writing
An eBook and eBook Marketing

Robert K. Teske

ISBN:1470080206
ISBN- 13:9781470080204

DEDICATION

This is dedicated to everyone who has ever wanted to write an eBook about anything but don't have the foggiest idea of what an eBook is or where to even start.

And this is especially dedicated to the unsung heroes who have fought and given their all to keep this great country of ours Free.

To the Men and Women of the United States Armed Forces.

And to the United States of America.

CONTENTS

ACKNOWLEDGMENTS

I would like to acknowledge everyone who has believed in me.

CHAPTER 1

Why write an eBook?

It's not true that everything that has been said has already been written. Since that unfortunate axiom came into use, the whole universe has changed. Technology has changed, ideas have changed, and the mindsets of entire nations have changed.

The fact is that this is the perfect time to write an eBook. What the publishing industry needs are people who can tap into the world as it is today – innovative thinkers who can make the leap into the new millennium and figure out how to solve old problems in a new way.

eBooks are a new and powerful tool for original thinkers with fresh ideas to disseminate information to the millions of people who are struggling to figure out how to do a plethora of different things.

Let's say you already have a brilliant idea, and the knowledge to back it up that will enable you to write an exceptional eBook. You may be sitting at your computer staring at a blank screen wondering, "Why? Why should I go through all the trouble of writing my eBook when it's so impossible to get anything published these days?

Well, let me assure you that publishing an eBook is entirely different than publishing a book in print. Let's look at the specifics of how the print and cyber publishing industry differ, and the many reasons why you should take the plunge and get your fingers tapping across those keyboards!

Submitting a print book to conventional publishing houses or to agents is similar to wearing a hair shirt 24/7. No matter how good your book actually is, or how many critique services and mentor writers have told you that "you've got what it takes," your submitted manuscript keeps coming back to you as if it is a boomerang instead of a valuable mine of information.

Perhaps, in desperation, you've checked out self-publishing and found out just how expensive a venture it can be. Most "vanity presses" require minimal print runs of at least 500 copies, and even that amount will cost you thousands of dollars. Some presses' minimal run starts at 1,000 to 2,000 copies.

And that's just for the printing and binding. Add in distribution, shipping, and promotional costs and - well, you do the math. Even if you wanted to go this route, you may not have that kind of money to risk.

Let's say you already have an Internet business with a quality website and a quality product. An eBook is one of the most powerful ways to promote your business while educating people with the knowledge you already possess as a business owner of a specific product or service.

For example, let's say that you've spent the last twenty-five years growing and training bonsai trees, and now you're ready to share your knowledge and experience. An eBook is the perfect way to reach the largest audience of bonsai enthusiasts.

eBooks will not only promote your business - they will help you make a name for yourself and your company, and establish you as an expert in your field. You may even find that you have enough to say to warrant a series of eBooks. Specific businesses are complicated and often require the different aspects to be divided in order for the reader to get the full story.

Perhaps your goals are more finely tuned in terms of the eBook scene. You may want to build a whole business around writing and publishing eBooks. Essentially, you want to start an e-business. You are thinking of setting up a website to promote and market your eBooks. Maybe you're even thinking of producing an ezine.

One of the most prevalent reasons people read eBooks is to find information about how to turn their Internet businesses into a profit-making machine. And these people are looking to the writers of eBooks to provide them with new ideas and strategies because writers of eBooks are usually people who understand the new cyberspace world we now live in. eBook writers are experts in Internet marketing campaigns and the strategies of promoting and distributing eBooks. The cyberspace community needs its eBooks to be successful so that more and more eBooks will be written.

You may want to create affiliate programs that will also market your eBook. Affiliates can be people or businesses worldwide that will all be working to sell your eBooks. Think about this? Do you see a formula for success here?

Figure out what your subject matter is, and then narrow it down. Your goal is to aim for specificity. Research what's out there already, and try to find a void that your eBook might fill.

What about an eBook about a wedding cake business? Or an eBook about caring for elderly pets? How about the fine points of collecting ancient pottery?

You don't have to have three masters degrees to write about your subject. People need advice that is easy to read and easily understood. Parents need advice for dealing with their teenagers. College students need to learn good study skills - quickly. The possibilities are endless.

After you've written your eBook

Getting your eBook out is going to be your focus once you've finished writing it, just as it is with print books. People will hesitate to buy any book from an author they've never heard of. Wouldn't you?

The answer is simple: give it away! You will see profits in the form of promoting your own business and getting your name out. You will find affiliates who will ask you to place their links within your eBook, and these affiliates will in turn go out and make your name known. Almost every single famous eBook author has started out this way.

Another powerful tool to attract people to your eBook is to make it interactive. Invent something for them to do within the book rather than just producing pages that contain static text. Let your readers fill out questionnaires, forms, even crossword puzzles geared to testing their knowledge on a particular subject.

Have your readers hit a link that will allow them to recommend your book to their friends and associates. Or include an actual order form so at the end of their reading journey, they can eagerly buy your product.

When people interact with books, they become a part of the world of that book. The fact is just as true for books in print as it is for eBooks.

That's why eBooks are so essential. Not only do they provide a forum for people to learn and make sense of their own thoughts, but they can also serve to promote your business at the same time.

CHAPTER 2

How to Write an Ebook

The hardest part of writing is the first sentence. When you look at the whole project, it seems like an impossible task. That's why you have to break it down into manageable tasks. Think of climbing a mountain. You are standing at the foot of it and looking up at its summit vanishing into the clouds. How can you possibly scale such an immense and dangerous mountain?

There is only one way to climb a mountain ? step by step.

Now think of writing your eBook in the same light. You must create it step by step, and one day, you will take that last step and find yourself standing on the summit with your head in the clouds.

The first thing you have to do, as if you actually were a mountain climber, is to get organized. Instead of climbing gear, however, you must organize your thoughts. There are some steps you should take before you begin. Once you've gone through the following list, you will be ready to actually begin writing your eBook.

Beginning Steps to Writing an eBook

First, figure out your e-Book's working title. Jot down a few different titles, and eventually, you'll find that one that will grow on you. Titles help you to focus your writing on your topic; they guide you in anticipating and answering your reader's queries. Many non-fiction books also have subtitles. Aim for clarity in your titles, but cleverness always helps to sell books ? as long as it's not too cute. For example, ***Remedies for Insomnia: twenty different ways to count sheep***. Or: Get off that couch: fifteen exercise plans to whip you into shape.

Next, write out a thesis statement. Your thesis is a sentence or two stating exactly what problem you are addressing and how your book will solve that problem. All chapters spring forth from your thesis statement.

Once you've got your thesis statement fine-tuned, you've built your foundation. From that foundation, your book will grow, chapter by chapter.

Your thesis will keep you focused while you write your eBook. Remember: all chapters must support your thesis statement. If they don't, they don't belong in your book. For example, your thesis statement could read:

> ***We've all experienced insomnia at times in our lives, but there are twenty proven techniques and methods to give you back a good night's sleep.***

Once you have your thesis, before you start to write, make sure there is a good reason to write your book. Ask yourself some questions:

- Does your book present useful information and is that information currently relevant?

- Will you book positively affect the lives of your readers?

- Is your book dynamic and will it keep the reader's attention?

- Does you book answer questions that are meaningful and significant?

If you can answer yes to these questions, you can feel confident about the potential of your eBook.

Another important step is to figure out who your target audience is. It is this group of people you will be writing to, and this group will dictate many elements of your book, such as style, tone, diction, and even length. Figure out the age range of your readers, their general gender, what they are most interested in, and even the socio-economic group they primarily come from. Are they people who read fashion magazines or book reviews? Do they write letters in longhand or spend hours every day online. The more you can pin down your target audience, the easier it will be to write your book for them.

Next, make a list of the reasons you are writing your eBook. Do you want to promote your business? Do you want to bring quality traffic to your website? Do you want to enhance your reputation?

Then write down your goals in terms of publishing. Do you want to sell it as a product on your website, or do you want to offer it as a free gift for filling out a survey or for ordering a product? Do you want to use the chapters to create an e-course, or use your eBook to attract affiliates around the world? The more you know upfront, the easier the actual writing will be.

Decide on the format of your chapters. In non-fiction, keep the format from chapter to chapter fairly consistent. Perhaps you plan to use an introduction to your chapter topic, and then divide it into four subhead topics. Or you may plan to divide it into five parts, each one beginning with a relevant anecdote.

How to make your eBook "user friendly"

You must figure out how to keep your writing engaging. Often anecdotes, testimonials, little stories, photos, graphs, advice, and tips will keep the reader turning the pages. Sidebars are useful for quick, accessible information, and they break up the density of the page.

Write with a casual, conversational tone rather than a formal tone such as textbook diction. Reader's respond to the feeling that you are having a conversation with them. Break up the length and structure of your sentences so you don't hypnotize your readers into sleep. Sentences that are all the same length and structure tend to be a good aid for insomnia!

Good writing takes practice. It takes lots and lots of practice. Make a schedule to write at least a page a day. Read books and magazines about the process of writing, and jot down tips that jump out at you. The art of writing is a lifetime process; the more you write (and read), the better your writing will become. The better your writing becomes, the bigger your sales figures.

In an eBook that is read on the screen, be aware that you must give your reader's eye a break. You can do this by utilizing white space. In art classes, white space is usually referred to as "negative space." Reader's eyes need to rest in the cool white oasis's you create on your page. If your page is too dense, your reader will quit out of it as soon as their eyes begin to tear.

Make use of lists, both bulleted and numbered. This makes your information easy to absorb, and gives the reader a mental break from dissecting your paragraphs one after the other.

Finally, decide on an easy-to-read design. Find a font that's easy on the eyes, and stick to that font family. Using dozens of fonts will only tire your readers out before they've gotten past your introduction. Use at least one and a half line spacing, and text large enough to be read easily on the screen, but small enough so that the whole page can be seen on a computer screen. You will have to experiment with this to find the right combination.

Of course, don't forget to run a spell and grammar check. You are judged by something as minor as correct punctuation, so don't mess up a great book by tossing out semicolons randomly, or stringing sentences together with commas. (By the way, that's called a "comma splice.")

Last of all, create an index and a bibliography. That's it! You've written a book! Now all you have to do is publish your eBook online, and wait for download request from your website visitors.

CHAPTER 3

Overcoming Writer's Block

What is writer's block?

Well, I just can't think of a single darn thing to say. Oh well, I'm out of here!

Sound familiar? No! Oh, get real! We've all experienced this phenomenon when we absolutely have to write something, particularly on deadline. I'm talking about. . . . .uh, I can't think of what the word is . . . oh, yes, it's on the tip of my tongue . . . it's:

WRITER'S BLOCK!!!!

Whew! I feel better just getting that out of my head and onto the page!

Writer's block is the patron demon of the blank page. You may think you know EXACTLY what you're going to write, but as soon as that evil white screen appears before you, your mind suddenly goes completely blank. I'm not talking about Zen meditation stare-at-the-wall-until-enlightenment-hits kind of blank.

I'm talking about sweat trickling down the back of your neck, anguish and panic and suffering kind of blank. The tighter the deadline, the worse the anguish of writer's block gets.

Having said that, let me say it again. "The tighter the deadline, the worse the anguish of writer's block gets." Now, can you figure out what might possibly be causing this horrible plunge into speechlessness?

The answer is obvious: FEAR! You are terrified of that blank page. You are terrified you have absolutely nothing of value to say. You are afraid of the fear of writer's block itself!

It doesn't necessarily matter if you've done a decade of research and all you have to do is string sentences you can repeat in your sleep together into coherent paragraphs. Writer's block can strike anyone at any time. Based in fear, it raises our doubts about our own self-worth, but it's sneaky. It's writer's block, after all, so it doesn't just come and let you know that. No, it makes you feel like an idiot who just had your frontal lobes removed through your sinuses. If you dared to put forth words into the greater world, they would surely come out as gibberish!

Let's try and be rational with this irrational demon. Let's make a list of what might possibly be beneath this terrible and terrifying condition.

     1. Perfectionism. You must absolutely produce a masterpiece of literature straight off in the first draft. Otherwise, you qualify as a complete failure.

2. Editing instead of composing. There's your monkey-mind sitting on your shoulder, yelling as soon as you type "I was born?," no, not that, that's wrong! That's stupid! Correct correct correct correct?

3. Self-consciousness. How can you think, let alone write, when all you can manage to do is pry the fingers of writer's block away from your throat enough so you can gasp in a few shallow breaths? You're not focusing on what you're trying to write, your focusing on those gnarly fingers around your windpipe.

4. Can't get started. It's always the first sentence that's the hardest. As writers, we all know how EXTREMELY important the first sentence is. It must be brilliant! It must be unique! It must hook your reader's from the start! There's no way we can get into writing the piece until we get past this impossible first sentence.

5. Shattered concentration. You're cat is sick. You suspect your mate is cheating on you. Your electricity might be turned off any second. You have a crush on the local UPS deliveryman. You have a dinner party planned for your in-laws. You . . . Need I say more. How can you possibly concentrate with all this mental clutter?

6. Procrastination. It's your favorite hobby. It's your soul mate. It's the reason you've knitted 60 argyle sweaters or made 300 bookcases in your garage workshop. It's the reason you never run out of Brie.

FACE IT, IT'S ONE OF THE REASONS YOU HAVE WRITER'S BLOCK!

How to Overcome Writer's Block

Okay. I can hear that herd of you running away from this chapter as fast as you can. Absurd! you huff. Never in a million years, you fume. Writer's block is absolutely, undeniably, scientifically proven to be impossible to overcome.

Oh, just get over it! Well, I guess it's not that easy. So try to sit down for just a few minutes and listen. All you have to do is listen ? you don't have to actually write a single word.

Ah, there you all are again. I am beginning to make you out now that the cloud of dust is settling.

I am here to tell you that:

WRITER'S BLOCK CAN BE OVERCOME.

Please, remain seated.

There are ways to trick this nasty demon. Pick one, pick several, and give them a try. Soon, before you even have a chance for your heartbeat to accelerate, guess what? You're writing.

Here are some tried and true methods of overcoming writer's block:

1. Be prepared. The only thing to fear is fear itself. (I know, that's a cliché but as soon as you start writing, feel free to improve on it.) If you spend some time mulling over your project before you actually sit down to write, you may be able to circumvent the worst of the crippling panic.

2. Forget perfectionism. No one ever writes a masterpiece in the first draft. Don't put any expectations on your writing at all! In fact, tell yourself you're going to write absolute garbage, and then give yourself permission to happily stink up your writing room.

3. Compose instead of editing. Never, never write your first draft with your monkey-mind sitting on your shoulder making snide editorial comments. Composing is a magical process. It surpasses the conscious mind by galaxies. It's even incomprehensible to the conscious, editorial, monkey-mind. So prepare an ambush. Sit down at your computer or your desk. Take a deep breath and blow out all your thoughts. Let your finger hover over your keyboard or pick up your pen. And then pull a fake: appear to be about to begin to write, but instead, using your thumb and index finger of your dominant hand, flick that little annoying ugly monkey back into the barrel of laughs it came from. Then jump in quickly! Write, scribble, scream, howl, let everything loose, as long as you do it with a pen or your computer keyboard.

4. Forget the first sentence. You can sweat over that all-important one-liner when you've finished your piece. Skip it! Go for the middle or even the end. Start wherever you can. Chances are, when you read it over, the first line will be blinking its little neon lights right at you from the depths of your composition.

5. Concentration. This is a hard one. Life throws us so many curve balls. How about thinking about your writing time as a little vacation from all those annoying worries. Banish them! Create a space, perhaps even a physical one, where nothing exists except the single present moment. If one of those irritating worries gets by you, stomp on it like you would an ugly bug!

6. Stop procrastinating. Write an outline. Keep your research notes within sight. Use someone else's writing to get going. Babble incoherently on paper or on the computer if you have to.

Just do it! (I know I stole that line from somewhere?). Tack up anything that could possibly help you to get going: notes, outlines, pictures of your grandmother. Put the cookie you will be allowed to eat when you finish your first draft within sight ? but out of reach. Then pick up the same type of writing that you need to write, and read it. Then read it again. Soon, trust me, the fear will slowly fade away. As soon as it does, grab your keyboard ? and get writing!

CHAPTER 4

Choosing an EBook Compiler

What is an eBook compiler?

You've written and revised your eBook, hired an artist who has produced outstanding graphics, and now you're ready to actually put together your eBook. What you need to make an eBook is software called an eBook Compiler.

There are many different compilers to chose from, but first, you need to know exactly what an eBook Compiler does. Here is the simple explanation:

An eBook compiler is a software program that converts either text pages or HTML text into a single executable file or an eBook.

If you or someone you hired has created a file with graphics in HTML, you will need an HTML eBook Compiler. This type of compiler requires a working knowledge of the HTML tag language. You can also use software to do this for you, such as Microsoft FrontPage or Macromedia Dreamweaver.

How do you choose an eBook Compiler?

There are a large number of eBook Compilers available on the market, all with glowing sales copy and tekkie language. It can get very confusing and overwhelming very fast without some simple guidelines to help you figure out which compiler is right for you.

Choosing an eBook Compiler depends on a number of factors:

1. How did you create your pages? Did you use HTML or PDF format? There are many more compilers available for HTML, but you can find some very good compilers that will covert your PDF files into an eBook.

2. Consider how easy the program is to use and the thoroughness of the software's instruction manual. It is absolutely necessary that the compiler you buy have an instructional manual, documentation, or online "wizards." If it doesn't, your chances of figuring out how to correctly use the program are compromised, and the time required doing so is going to be significant.

Many manufacturers of compilers offer a free trial version so you can play around with it and see if it suits your needs. Download the trial version and ascertain that it actually does what it claims to do.

3. Security features. If you plan to sell your eBook, check out the security features of the compiler software carefully. Security features should include: prevention of the reader from modifying text, access only to the pages you assign or by entering a password, different ways of generating passwords such as secure passwords, user-friendly, and open passwords.

4. Supported scripting. Find out what scripts the software supports. Scripting allows you to create special effects, customize menus, and create and modify other user interactivity. Choose a compiler that permits you to include graphics, search windows, hyperlinks, forms, surveys, etc.

5. Pricing. This is a factor that is not always easy to gauge. The highest priced compilers are not automatically your best choice. Choose your compiler based on the necessary requirements for your eBook. That means you need to know exactly how you plan to use your eBook and what functions you require.

Let's look at some of these factors in more detail. First of all, make sure you have the correct browser to run the compiler. The majority of HTML compilers use Microsoft Internet Explorer or Netscape. Check out the version that the compiler supports. Compilers that require a browser will not run on a computer that does not have the required browser installed. However, there are eBook HTML compilers that don't require you to have any browser installed on your computer. These compilers run on any Windows system.

If you choose a compiler that requires a browser, check to ascertain that the browser is installed correctly and that it is properly configured to the specifications of the compiler. Check to see if certain functions are turned off or on, and make any adjustments according to the compiler instructions.

Security is an essential element of any compiler, regardless of whether you plan to sell or give away your eBook. One of the main reasons for using a compiler is to prevent the reader from modifying the contents. A secure compiler allows access only to the pages you want the user to access unless they enter a correct password.

To find out how secure an eBook HTML compiler is, open an eBook on it. While it is open, check the temporary directory of your computer. This can usually be accessed by typing in C:\Windows\temp. If you see a bunch of files when your eBook is open or running, it means that your computer is decompressing the secure data from your eBook before showing the eBook to the viewer. This method is not secure! It means that anyone with the knowledge of how to access these temporary files can steal the secure data and then they can fiddle with your eBook to their evil heart's desire. Remember, one of the main purposes of buying and using an HTML compiler is to protect your property.

Next, let's discuss passwords. When trying to choose an eBook Compiler, check out the type of passwords that the compiler supports. Almost all compilers offer some kind of password protection that insures that the user can only access the contents they have purchased from you. However, the best compilers offer varied ways to generate different types of passwords. Choose a compiler that gives you the options of secure, user-friendly, and open password generation.

Another important factor when it comes to passwords is how the compiler generates them. A compiler that has internal password protection generation built into the software is more secure than compilers that link to live Internet password control systems.

Find out if the compiler generates passwords online. If it has this option, it allows you to choose any payment processing system you want or to do the payment processing yourself.

Next, look into the size of eBook the compiler supports. The best compilers can create eBooks up to 2 GB in size without decompressing the HTML pages or images to your hard disk. Usually, ebooks that are 2 GB in size can easily support 6 GB of compressed data. The catch here is that only text files will generally be compressible.

You do not want a compiler that decompresses this amount of data when the user attempts to open your eBook. This would mean that anyone who purchases your eBook will have to wait for all the data to decompress before they can access your eBook right after downloading it. So look for compilers that only decompress temporarily files that are NOT HTML to the local hard-disk. Non-HTML files include Flash, Word, and Acrobat files. This type of compiler is more secure and certainly faster.

Make sure the compiler you choose is compatible with your system software. Check out what version of Windows it requires, and make sure you have that version before buying your compiler.

Support issues are extremely important. Choose a compiler that includes an installation program. This program allows your user to choose a number of different places on their computer to install the eBook, to place a shortcut on their desktop, and to add the ebook, if they choose, to the Start Programs menu.

You also want excellent and accessible vendor support. Make sure you can access quick technical support! At three o'clock in the morning, this factor will be VERY important. Also, check to see the terms of free technical support offered. Unlimited technical support is obviously the best option.

Check to see if the company that puts out the compiler software offers a service level agreement. This agreement is to assure you of their quality response to your questions or problems.

A good thing to consider is how long the compiler has been on the market. Usually, the version number will give you an idea. The longer the program is on the market, the higher the version number, the more bugs have been worked out.

When choosing an eBook compiler, do not be swayed by incredible promises and dazzling sales copy. Do your homework first, and then consider all the above issues and factors before choosing an eBook compiler.

CHAPTER 5

Rating eBook Compilers

Now that you've finished writing your eBook and have a basic understanding of what an eBook compiler does, you may be feeling overwhelmed by the number of compilers on the market. To help you make your decision, I have tested and reviewed the best-rated eBook compilers currently available.

* E-ditor

This software has a demo version that you can download to try out before purchasing. You can't actually use the demo to create an eBook, but you can run the software and test it out thoroughly to see if it does what you need it to do for your particular eBook.

This eBook compiler is one of the easiest to use. The software has a very user-friendly help menu that provides instructions for and explanations of every field on every screen. The program also includes video tutorials demonstrating every step of this compiler with clear explanations of all fields that need to be filled out. There are 7 screens that you use to choose your eBook options.

This compiler requires your files to be in HTML format. You follow simple directions, and the compiler loads your files. If you decide to edit your eBook after it has been compiled, make any changes in your original files and click on "Compile you eBook" and your changes will appear in your compiled eBook.

E-editor allows for some customization of your eBook. You can create a special page that appears when the eBook is opened; create customized icons that appear on the desktop after downloading; use your own logo on the task bar of your eBook; customize the task bar's buttons, where the task bar appears in your eBook, and choose the task bar's colors. Additionally, you can choose to have the eBook open to the last page read, which many of your buyers will appreciate.

An excellent and unique feature of E-ditor is the capability to choose a standard Microsoft window or to create your own design for a window to personalize your eBook. The program provides some sample window designs, but you can use any .bmp (bit map skin) graphic you have stored on your hard drive.

E-ditor is a good choice if you are new at producing eBooks because it is easy to use and allows you to customize the appearance of your eBook.

* Desktop Author

This compiler does not require a browser, nor do you have to download software or plug-ins. The program converts exe. files into pages that look like a standard book. You can create and produce eBook pages scaled to fit on your computer screen without any scrolling. Additional features include WYSIWGY (what you see is what you get) page editing and creation, the ability to manipulate internal images, cut and paste functions, hotlinks to pages, email, website, or other files. It is an excellent compiler to use for a marketing tools, such as creating brochures and manuals in addition to eBooks.

* EBook Edit Pro

This compiler provides a demo version, which allows you to test out its features. The software uses a Wizard that leads you step-by-step through the set-up and creation of your eBook. Customization includes text editing that appears on the pop-up starting message window; the ability to allow or prevent resizing of your book and the mouse-click pop-up menu; enabling or disabling the navigation bar and choosing the buttons you want to appear; and customizing the e-Book's desktop icon and the logo that appears on the navigation bar.

eBook Edit Pro is loaded with excellent features that allow you to create multi-media eBooks, and includes a Wizard that is customized for beginners and for advanced users. The software uses HTML files, downloading them from the directory where they are saved. Edit and resave your files in the original software used to create those files, and then with a single click you can re-compile your eBook.

Features include customization of icons, toolbars, and the "about box." This compiler has a particularly useful feature called the Rebrander feature. This permits you to enter customized code into your eBook pages and distribute the Rebrander software to your affiliates or distributors. They can then customize the links included in the eBook, but they can not alter any link or information that you have not entered a customized code for.

The software includes "eBrand-It" software that allows custom fields for your customer's name, affiliate ID or URL. This feature is a powerful marketing tool because affiliates are much happier giving away your eBook from their own site when they can customize it.

* eBook Compiler

This compiler offers a demo version that allows you to compile 10 files. If you don't include graphics, you can create a 10 page eBook that allows printing and copying of the eBook. The catch is that you can't sell any eBook you create in the demo version.

The purchased software is user-friendly with easy-to-follow help files that not only guide you through the steps of compiling your eBook, but also explains what an eBook compiler does. The software provides detailed instructions on how to create source files from Microsoft Word 2000 and 1997, PowerPoint 2000 and 1997, and HTML documents. It contains less detailed instructions for creating source files from other programs.

This compiler allows for password protection of your entire eBook or for selected pages. Additionally, you can set a time limit on your eBook. When the runs out, the customer no longer has access unless they pay for it. In other words, it allows you to create a demo version of your eBook for marketing purposes.

You can set a single password or multiple passwords. Using multiple passwords assigns each user their own specific password. Online help files guide you through setting up your passwords. You can also create a Sales and Thank-you page for selling a password protected eBook. This is a good choice for the novice, particularly since it includes basic features for password protection and distribution.

* Activ Ebook Compiler

This is an easy to use compiler that provides excellent features. This software can support HTML, JPEG, GIF, and all active plug-ins. Features includes password protection, branding, internet linking, icon customization, assigning unique serial numbers, splash screen, file compression, and start-up messages. It also provides free lifetime upgrades. Additionally, it includes a preprocessor, re-brander, active script, and detailed instructions for using HTML, Power Point, and Microsoft Word files.

There are several other excellent Ebook compilers on the market that are worth looking into.

Ebook Generator features splash screens, password protection, branding, icon customization, and compression control. Additionally, it includes virus prevention that alerts the user to any modifications made to your Ebook and offers usage statistics so you can track your eBook's use. With all these advanced features, this is an excellent compiler for the beginner because it is exceptionally easy to run.

Ebook Creator is another excellent compiler, supporting HTML, JPEG, GIF, and PNG graphics, and JavaScript, VB script, and Java applets. It also supports all Internet Explorer plug-ins. Standard features include unique serial numbers, direct linking to a form or a page on your website, disabled right clicking, and search functions. The software allows for expiration after a set number of days or usages, which allows you to create demo versions. You can create up to 1000 different passwords; every time the Ebook is downloaded, a unique password is required to access protected pages. The software provides user-friendly menus and buttons that allow the beginner to the advanced user to easily create their Ebook.

Obviously, there are some excellent compilers out there. So figure out EVERYTHING you need in terms of features, and then compare prices and options. Do take advantage of demo versions if they are offered before purchasing. And then, have fun creating your Ebook!

CHAPTER 6

Steps to Publishing Success

Even if your best friend owns a top publishing company, giving you an immediate "in," this does not guarantee publishing success.

First, you have to write a quality book that has a clear target audience. And your book must answer a common problem or need that audience shares. Then you have to develop a marketing plan, and stick to it for at least two years.

Let's begin with the process that should commence before you write your first word. Begin by reading A LOT. Read both books you passionately love and books you can't seem to make it past page five. Then figure out what the author did in the book you loved, and what was wrong with in the book you couldn't finish. Write down these points so they are crystal clear to you. Read other people's books for inspiration and to discover what you should avoid as a writer.

The next step is to plan out your book. Narrow down your subject, and then divide it into chapters. Each chapter should address a specific aspect of the problem your book is going to solve. In each chapter, break the specific aspect down into several parts. This will help your readers take in your information a bit at a time instead of overwhelming them with every bit of information clogging up the pages until they feel like they're about to go blind. It's not quite spoon-feeding the information to your readers, but it's close.

The next two steps are obvious. Write your book and then revise it. And then revise it again. And perhaps again. Of course, writing is extremely hard, and writing a book can seem like an impossible task. There are many books out there that give you guidelines to help you become familiar - and even love - the process of writing and revision. Find a number of books about writing. Better yet, find a number of books about writing the specific type of book you aspire to write. These can serve as roadmaps on your writing journey.

Once you've written your eBook and revised it at least twice, show it to someone else whose opinion you respect. If you're lucky enough to know a good editor, see if you have something to barter for him or her to go through your manuscript. Or join a writing group and let the other members critique your work.

Then take all these ideas from other people, and revise your manuscript one last time. And then stop! Put down that pen! Get your hands off the keyboard!

One of the most important steps to actually producing a book is to know when to stop writing and tinkering with it.

You've finally written your eBook! Pop open the bubbly! Give yourself a night out on the town!

Okay, now that this necessary celebration is out of your system, what do you do next?

How to turn your eBook into Profits

eBooks are a revolutionary way to publish your book without incurring the costs of print production. All you need is a relevant and targeted subject and some inexpensive software, and you can transform your manuscript into a book.

The problem, in terms of actually seeing any profits from your eBook, is that the market is overwhelmed with eBooks, and many of them are not worth the time it takes to download them. Just because the ability exists to easily produce an eBook, doesn't make it good writing.

Make sure your book does not simply rehash old material. You will injure your credibility as an author by claiming to offer valuable new insights and disappointing your audience with material they've read a zillion times before. So spend enough time writing and revising your book to make sure it's of the highest quality and presents the most current information. A good book will eventually sell itself; false claims about your book will make it extremely difficult to sell any future books you may write.

Assuming you have determined that you do indeed have a quality product that answers some question or need of your target audience with NEW information, how do you know how much to charge for it? Rule number 1: Set a price for your book equal to its value. An under-priced book will only give the impression that your book isn't worth very much.

To figure out a fair price, estimate how much time you put into creating it and how difficult it was to transform the necessary information into understandable and engaging writing. Figure out how much your time and effort is worth, and then price it accordingly. The goal is for you to be adequately compensated for your talent, your time, and your effort.

Once you've figured out a price that is high enough to convey the value of the book, but not so high as to be out of the reach of your target audience's mean budget, then it's time to offer it for sale on your website. To attract sales, you will need to develop a promotional campaign, particularly if you are an unknown author.

There are multitudes of books about self-promotion that will guide you in your efforts. Choose a plan that is both creative and professional. Learn how to write a catchy yet informative press release, and send copies of your eBook to sites that specialize in eBook reviews.

Learn how to write powerful sales copy, or hire someone to write it for you. This is an essential. You absolutely need excellent sales copy to sell your book. Make sure the copy includes all the reasons your target audience needs your book, and the benefits they will derive from buying it.

Use graphics in your promotional materials. Beautiful graphics have the power to instantly convey the quality and value of your eBook. Graphics can also convey the amount of valuable information the book contains, and your careful attention to detail. Professional graphics sell professional books. They reassure the customer that the product is what it claims to be.

Consider excerpting chapters for articles. You can offer these tidbits for free on your website as a sort of demo of your book. Include an order form for your eBook at the end of the excerpted articles.

Finally, when you set-up your download link, make sure to simplify the process. It's a good idea to offer a few bonuses that make your book even more enticing to purchase, but make sure the bonuses are valuable and high quality. Too many bonuses that are basically a load of useless stuff will compromise the impression your audience has of your eBook. The goal is to convey to your audience that they are getting a quality product for a good deal. That means applying restraint, especially when it comes to adding bonus items. Too much free stuff offered diminishes your credibility.

Make sure your book is a quality product. Make sure it is relevant and current. Develop an effective marketing plan that includes excellent sales copy and excerpted articles. Then offer your book for sale, and wait for your audience to discover you!

CHAPTER 7

How to Price Your eBook

You've written and compiled an eBook. Now you have to decide how much to charge for it. Finding the right price is essential to the success of your product. If you charge too little, people will think it's of little value, and they won't purchase it, or even it they do buy your book, you will have to sell thousands of copies to get to the point where you can begin to see a profit. If you price it too high when compared with your competition, you will find yourself steadily lowering the price, which will cause you all kinds of new problems in the future. For example, if you sell your eBook at first for $39.99, and later reduce it to $24.95, don't you think the people who bought it for $39.99 are going to be somewhat unhappy with you, to put it mildly?

Choosing the right price for your eBook is one of the most critical parts of the marketing process. The first rule of pricing eBooks is to never under price. Determine the highest price your audience can afford, and then if you find your book isn't selling, you can always reduce the price. Before you take that step, make sure you are promoting your book like crazy on the Internet and on websites. The price should be aimed at bringing in profits, but you should never forget that price is one of the factors that people use in judging the value of your eBook before they buy it. So always start with the highest price, and then launch a mega-marketing campaign.

Pricing an eBook is particularly difficult because eBooks are a fairly new commodity. Since they are digital, the value of an eBook is as confusing as the understanding of what digital actually is to the average layperson. This means that we must look at eBooks in a different light in order to determine their actual worth in this brave, new cyber world.

Let's look at the difference between a book in print and an eBook. A printed book is an object you can hold in your hand, store on your bookshelf, even hand down to the next generation. It is priced on factors such as paper stock, design and production costs, and marketing.

But the fact that unites eBooks and print books is that they are composed of ideas. It is the ideas in these books that have the ability to change, or possibly transform, people's lives.

What do you think an idea is worth when evaluated against the cost of paper and ink?

It is the IDEAS that are valuable! That is how you determine the cost of your eBook.

What should I charge for my ideas?

There are all different formulas and methods for determining the correct price for your eBook. Let's begin with honing in on your ultimate goals.

Decide if your goal is to get wide distribution and maximum exposure. This goal is aimed at drawing customers to your business or service, or to establishing the credibility of your reputation. If this is your main goal, you should aim to keep your price on the low side. Some authors have even priced their eBooks at a profit loss to draw a high number of new customers. The key is to find a price that maximizes your profits and the number of books you sell.

This is an excellent pricing strategy if you are looking to acquire long-term customers. Long-term customers are extremely likely to buy from you again and again ? as long as the first eBook they buy is of exceptional quality and beneficial to the customer.

However, if your book contains valuable, and more importantly NEW information, references, or techniques, then you should aim to price it on the high end.

After you figure out your goal, you must figure out what your audience's need is for your eBook. For example, does your book solve a particular problem? If it does, and solves it in a way that hasn't been written about in one hundred other eBooks, you will be able to achieve high sales at a high price. If your book solves a problem or answers questions in a new and unique way, you should price your book as high as you can go. You will achieve larger profits this way, but bring in fewer customers. Just make sure the question or problem that your book solves is one that is important and relevant to the majority of your market audience. If your ideas are not common knowledge, or you are presenting a brand new technique, you will be able to sell books at a high price. Just be prepared for your competition to undercut you on price as soon as they hear about your book.

Keep in mind that the above pricing strategy is temporary. Eventually, you will cease to sell books at this high price. So figure out in advance how long you plan to offer your eBook at this high price, and when that time is up, change your pricing strategy.

If you want to see large profits over customer draw, aim for an audience that is looking for easy solutions to their problems at a low price. If your book is aimed at solving one particular problem rather than general advice, then you can charge more. Start at the highest price the market will bear to bring in the largest profits, and plan to discount the book a number of times throughout the year.

Marketing Strategies

The key that unlocks the sales potential of your eBook is to find a single sentence that becomes your selling handle. This sentence states what question or problem your book answers and the benefits your eBook can provide. Then be sure to use that sentence in every piece of sales and promotional material, and every time anyone asks you about your eBook.

Besides promoting your books assiduously online, there are several other strategies that can help you sell more books.

One is to give something away for free with your book, such as a valuable bonus item. Or bundle several eBooks under one price, which lowers the price for each eBook if they were sold separately.

An effective technique for figuring out a price is to send out a survey to your current customers. If these customers have already bought an eBook from you, ask for their opinion in terms of price. Do this by creating a sales page for the new book, but don't include a price on that page. Instead, add a number of links to survey questions that ask pointed questions to aid you in assigning a price to your eBook.

Another strategy is to test out prices by creating a number of duplicate sales pages with different prices on each page. Make sure your sales copy is exactly the same on every page, and includes your selling-handle sentence. Then figure out for each page the conversion ratio between visitors to your site and sales of your book. This will tell you what your optimum price is.

Ultimately, if you've written a book that solves a problem or presents a new technique, your book will bring in both traffic and profits. So be sure to write that selling-handle sentence that sums up what problem your book solves and what the benefits of your book will be to the customers who purchase it. And then watch your market come to you!

CHAPTER 8 BONUS!!!

eBooks are Promotional Powerhouses

eBooks are part of the new frontier of cyberspace. They are an entirely new medium for sharing marketing information, ideas, techniques, and expert knowledge. Each day the number of people accessing the Internet grows, causing the exposure of your eBook to increase incrementally. It's obvious why electronic self-publishing has become so popular so quickly.

The publishing industry, I hope, does not intend to forever banish the printed word to the dustbin of history. Books in print have their own special qualities and merits, and the world would be diminished by their disappearance.

Having said that, let's look at what makes eBooks so important and so unique. eBooks have certain abilities and qualities that other mediums do not possess.

For example, eBooks are fairly easy to produce, and their production cost is inexpensive. Just think about it: you don't need a publisher, an agent, a printing press, offset film, ink, paper, or even a distributor. You just need a great concept, the ability to write it or to hire a writer, and the right software.

Additionally, eBooks are easily and rapidly distributed online. They are also easily updated; they do not require a second print run. All you need is to go into your original creation and modify the text or graphics. Because of this flexibility, eBooks can change and grow as fast as you can type.

eBooks are also immediately obtainable. You don't have to go to a bookstore or search through endless titles at an online bookstore. All you have to do is download it from a website, and presto! It's on your computer, ready to be read.

eBooks are interactive. This is one of the most unique and specific qualities that eBooks offer. You can add surveys that need to be filled out, order forms for customers to purchase your products or goods, sound and video that draw your reader into the virtual world of your eBook, even direct links to relevant sites that will expand your ebook outward. The potential is virtually limitless.

eBooks have a particular kind of permanence that other mediums do not possess. Television shows and radio shows air once, and then may rerun a few times. eBooks remain on your computer for as long as your choose, and they can be read and reread whenever you choose to. They can even be printed out and stored on the shelves of your traditional home library.

Another wonderful quality is that eBooks have no barriers in terms of publishing. You don't need to go through the endless process of submitting your manuscript over and over again, and then once you land an agent, having the agent submit your manuscript over and over again. Nor do you have to shell out thousands of dollars for printing a self-published book. All eBooks require is a writer and appropriate software. Figure out your market, write your book, post it on your website, and with the right business savvy, your audience will come to you.

Finally, you have creative control over your eBook. You don't have to compromise with an editor or the publishing trends of the time. You don't have to haggle with a designer or wait for copyedited galleys to arrive by snail mail. You are in complete control of the design and the text.

How to Use eBooks for Marketing and Promotion

There are innumerable ways to use eBooks to promote your business and drive quality traffic to your website. Once posted on your site, you can turn them into a daily course, which brings your customer back to read the next chapter. You can use them as a free gift for making a purchase or for filling out a survey. Put your eBook on a disc, and you will have an innovative brochure. Blow your competition away by inserting the disc into your sales packages.

The most effective marketing products are those that are unique. Copyright your eBook, and immediately, you have a powerful tool that you, and you alone, can offer to the public. People will have to visit your site to acquire your eBook, which increases the flow of quality traffic and the potential of sales and affiliate contacts.

Make sure that you keep your eBook current. Update it frequently as the market and trends change. Add new advice and techniques to show your prospects how your goods or services can enrich their lives. By constantly keeping abreast of new trends and techniques, you can continue to see profits from your eBook for years after your original creation.

Another phenomenal advantage of eBooks is that you can test their marketing potential without putting out hardly any cash at all. You can even produce an eBook one copy at a time, each time you receive an order, eliminating the need for storage and inventory. By this method, you can gauge the salability of your eBook, and make adjustments as necessary until the orders start pouring in. eBooks allow you to learn about your market and customer habits and motivation over a period of time, without risking your precious financial resources. They also provide you with an invaluable way to gather marketing information, which you can use in many different facets of your business.

Use your eBook to discover what the specific goals and problems are in your specific industry. Then figure out how to solve these problems, and publish an eBook with this invaluable information. This will increase the value of your business, upgrade your reputation, and get you known as an expert in your field.

You can extend the value of single eBook by breaking the book down into chapters for a serial course, into special reports available on your website, or into audio or visual tapes. eBooks can be broken down into several different promotional materials by excepting some of the articles and using them to promote your product. You can include a catalog in your eBook to promote all the products or services you sell. You can include a thank-you note for reading your book and an invitation to download a trial version of your product. Or you can include a form for your audience to contact you for further information or with questions, thereby building your business relationships and your mailing list.

Using eBooks in this manner helps to cut the cost of individually producing separate promotional materials. You can use a single eBook to entice new prospects and to sell new products to your current customers.

No other medium has this kind of flexibility and ability for expansion. Think of your eBook like a spider spinning a beautiful and intricate web. Now go and create that web, and see how many customers and prospects you can catch!

And now, with such outlets as CreateSpace.com, Amazon.com, and others for self-publishing, your options are only limited by your imagination. You can publish your eBook for sale on your website by using any number of eBook Compilers that I have covered, and even the ones that I haven't. Or, you can publish your work using CreateSpace.com and Amazon.com; and get your book in print and on Kindle, amongst other possibilities.

Now START WRITING and GET YOUR WORK OUT THERE!

Good Luck!

ABOUT THE AUTHOR

Robert K. Teske is currently CEO/Producer of Subtropolis Film Partners.

From January of 1975 to April 2008 Robert was the President and CEO of Teske Enterprises and was actively involved in the direct sales, direct mail, mail order, and Internet Marketing industries, the Security and Law Enforcement communities, as well as the entertainment industry as a speculative screenwriter. Since 1995 he has written several screenplays, and has had two television series proposals optioned. Subtropolis Film Partners was established in May 2008.

Teske graduated in 2008 from Dov S-S Simens' Hollywood Film Institute, Film School, and received both, a Producer's Diploma in the capacity of Feature Film Producer, and the Independent Filmmaker Certificate of Completion as a Certified Cinema Director & Line Producer, fulfilling a life-long desire to do so. He is currently resides in Kasson, Minnesota.